Table of Contents

Introduction

The purpose of this booklet is to explain in a step-by-step process how I put together two independent feature films for less than two thousand dollars on each project. The main reason that I decided to write this booklet is because many people often ask me how I did it. They know I am just a school teacher with dreams of making movies with no real money. Usually, the people asking me aren't aspiring filmmakers and they just want a simple answer. But the answer isn't simple. It's a process that has worked for me in which I had to learn through experience, and it can work for you also. How well it works really depends on you and how much you are willing to work in order to move your idea from a vision to an actual film. I have gone through this process twice, and it has worked both times. I have learned a lot from each experience, and I would have appreciated a guide like this one to help me along when I first began.

The good news is that you don't have to have a lot of money to make a good movie. If you have the drive to succeed and if you are determined to make a movie, it can be done with some basic planning. I hope that you find this booklet helpful in your quest to accomplish your dreams.

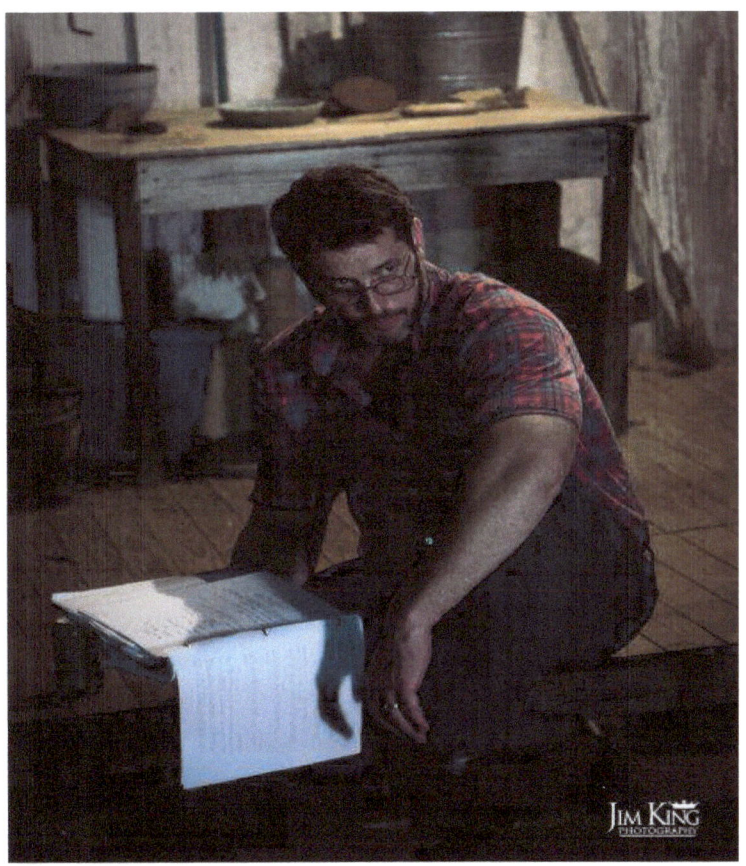

My Story

Ever since my dreams of playing Pro Football went up in smoke with a career ending injury in college, I have wanted to be a film actor and screenwriter in the movies. With the end of one dream came the birth of another. I knew nothing about movies at the time, only that I thought I could be an actor and also become a good writer if I was persistent over time. So it was in college that I began my journey to accomplish my other passion. It wasn't until years later, after several screenplays and many gigs as a movie extra, that I really started getting serious about my dream. Like all serious actors, I got an agent and started going to every audition I could, very rarely landing any roles. The main problem was that I was working as a teacher in the public schools and trying to take off for auditions during the school year. I don't know how many times my grandmother died in one year in order for me to leave for an important audition. I lost count. I don't recommend lying to take off for an audition by the way, but I can't say that I was always truthful with my employer in the beginning years of chasing the dream.

When I wasn't auditioning, I was writing. I was always working on the screenplay that I believed would be my ticket into the film industry. I was going to be like Sly Stallone, Matt Damon, or Tyler Perry. I was going to write my way into the industry and become this big, overnight success...but there was a problem; I couldn't sell any of my screenplays. I was submitting them to hundreds of production companies and getting hundreds of rejection letters.

The years started passing and the result was always the same. But I didn't give up on my dream. I kept writing and writing and writing. Then one day I submitted for a Christian Television writing gig in Waco, Texas for a company called "GodZone Ministries." They were making a shoestring budget sitcom called, "Heavenly High" that would air locally and on FaithTV. I knew nothing about writing for a sitcom, but thought I would give it a try. I ended up writing five episodes and becoming close friends with the Executive Producer of that show, Stuart. It wasn't long before Stuart and I had all these visions of grandeur of how we could find investors to make a feature length film, and how simple it could be if we just really tried our best.

Well, the second problem was finding an investor. Our sitcom series was low budget, and it was all we had to show potential investors. There weren't any investors wanting to invest 500k in a movie from unknown, wannabe filmmakers who had never made a movie before. Although at one point, we did come very close. We had a feature length film that was fully cast with recognizable talent attached to it. It was finally happening, or so we thought. Then a week before filming, the investor backed out and the production fell through. We were devastated; I was devastated. About a year passed and during that time I tried to find other investors to replace the one that backed out, but with no luck. I ran into the same problem as before; we didn't have anything to show that we could make a movie. We had no prior record of success.

Then one day, it just hit me. I give credit to God because I had prayed so many times for Him to show me the way and He did. *Why not write a movie that can be shot on a very low budget and do it in the summer when you aren't teaching at school?* It was an awesome idea. We could surely do this if we planned it right, and if it was even semi-successful then we could show potential investors what we did with little money. Maybe then they would fund one of our bigger projects. I talked it over with Stuart, my friend at GodZone, and he was all for it.

On set of "Preacher Man" our first feature film ; David Ford left. Stuart Miller right.

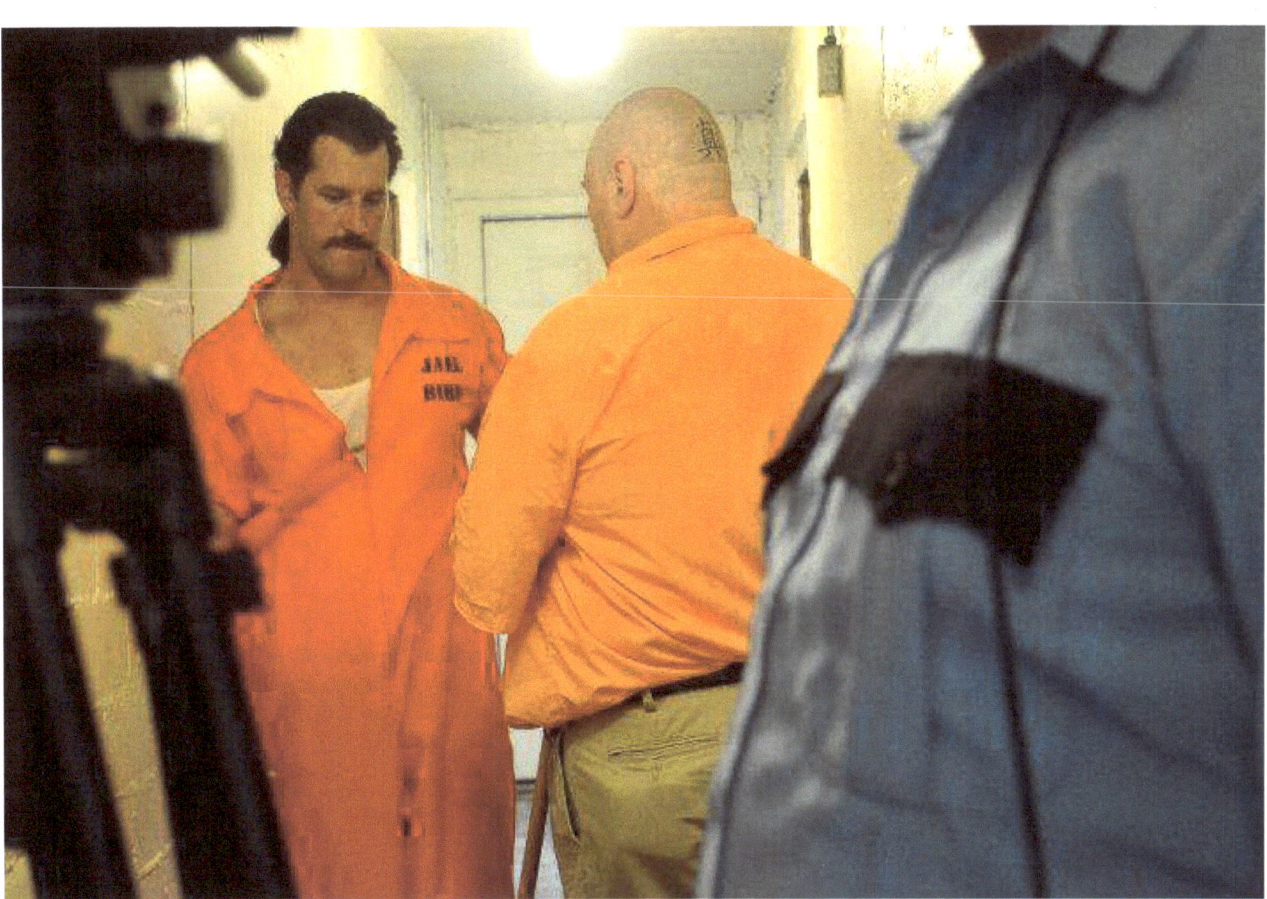

OUR FIRST FILM

The step-by-step outline that I am going to give you combines both our first and second film experiences. We learned most of the process through the first film, as well as made the biggest mistake. What is the big mistake we made, you may be wondering? I won't tell you just yet, because then the step-by-step outline would be out of order. When I get to that step in the process, I will give you all the gritty, little details so that you can be sure not to make the same mistake. It is a mistake that is still costing us to this day, one that put our first film into a legal struggle. It is the reason why that film is not yet released. The film is complete and our process of making a 200k film project for less than 2k worked to perfection, but there is a very important detail that we didn't think was a big deal at the time that came back to haunt us. Just because our first film isn't out in the market doesn't mean the process I am going to outline for you did not work. The process didn't fail us, we failed the process on our first film. We were sure not to repeat it on our second film.

Now, are you ready to begin the first step in the process?

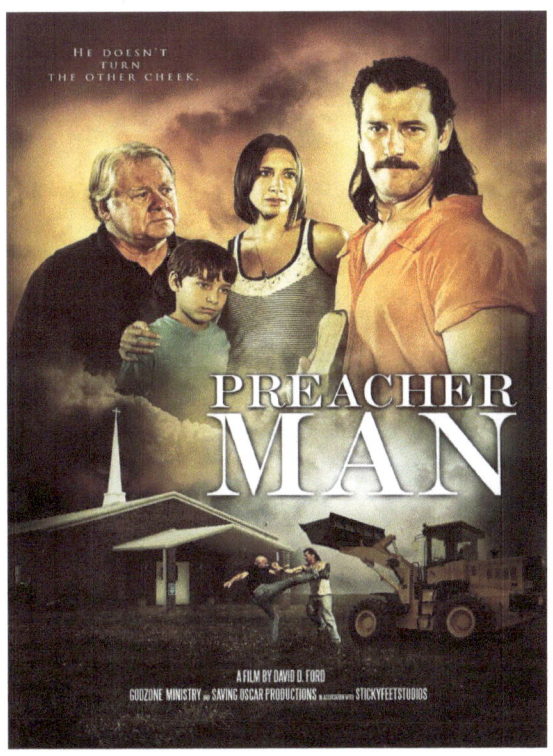

Poster for "Preacher Man"

STEP 1: THE SCRIPT

Before you can make a movie, you've got to have a screenplay. You don't have to be the writer of the screenplay, but you will need to have the rights to use that screenplay. This is the tricky part in this whole process because if you have a screenplay that cost a million or more to make, then this process will not work. You have to have a screenplay that can be done locally in your area that is **written for low budget filming.**

It is very important that you don't write or use a script that is unrealistic for the budget you're making your film on. For example, don't write an expensive car chase scene where three cars are totaled unless you can total three cars. Don't write a scene with a .747 crashing into a house unless you can afford high priced CGI effects. Instead, write something that is more feasible. It may be possible to write a car chase scene if you only have to total one car. Maybe you have an old clunker in the backyard that is only worth about a thousand dollars, and you are willing to crash it for an important scene. **The main point here is to develop a screenplay that you can realistically shoot without being out hard cash.** With some creativity and networking, you will be surprised what all you can accomplish.

In my first film, "Preacher Man," I needed an old jail cell for a scene. In our production office, which was an old church, they had part of the building condemned and locked up. I took a look inside, and it looked like it could be an old jail cell. So I had someone spray paint PVC pipes black and put them across the windows. We even made a door out of PVC pipe that looked just like an old jail cell door, reminiscent to the one on the Andy Griffith show. I could go on, but hopefully you understand the point here. If you currently do not have a screenplay that can be shot realistically for a shoestring budget, then you need to write one or have someone write one for you.

Next, while this is not a must when it comes to the process that I am outlining for you, it is important that the story is interesting and exciting. Just because it isn't a million dollar budget doesn't mean it can't be one of the best stories ever told. It would be a shame for you to go through this entire process and make a movie only to discover it is a film that nobody wants to see. Some of the best films ever made are indie films. So my advice to you is to make sure you have a story that can be shot on a shoestring budget and that your film is something that people will want to see.

In this part of the creative process, I can't really offer much advice because all writers must find their own writing style and unique voice. Take your time with the script, develop it, and think about locations that you can get when you write. When the time comes to shoot the film, it may not be as easy as you thought if you have to shut down two blocks of downtown Dallas. Yet shutting down a block in your local town for a couple hours with the help of the city council is far more realistic.

Section Highlights

1. The script must be written for low budget production.
2. Even a low budget script can be exciting. Make sure you have an interesting story that people will want to see. It may be much harder for this process to

work for you if the people that you're trying to get involved hate the story.

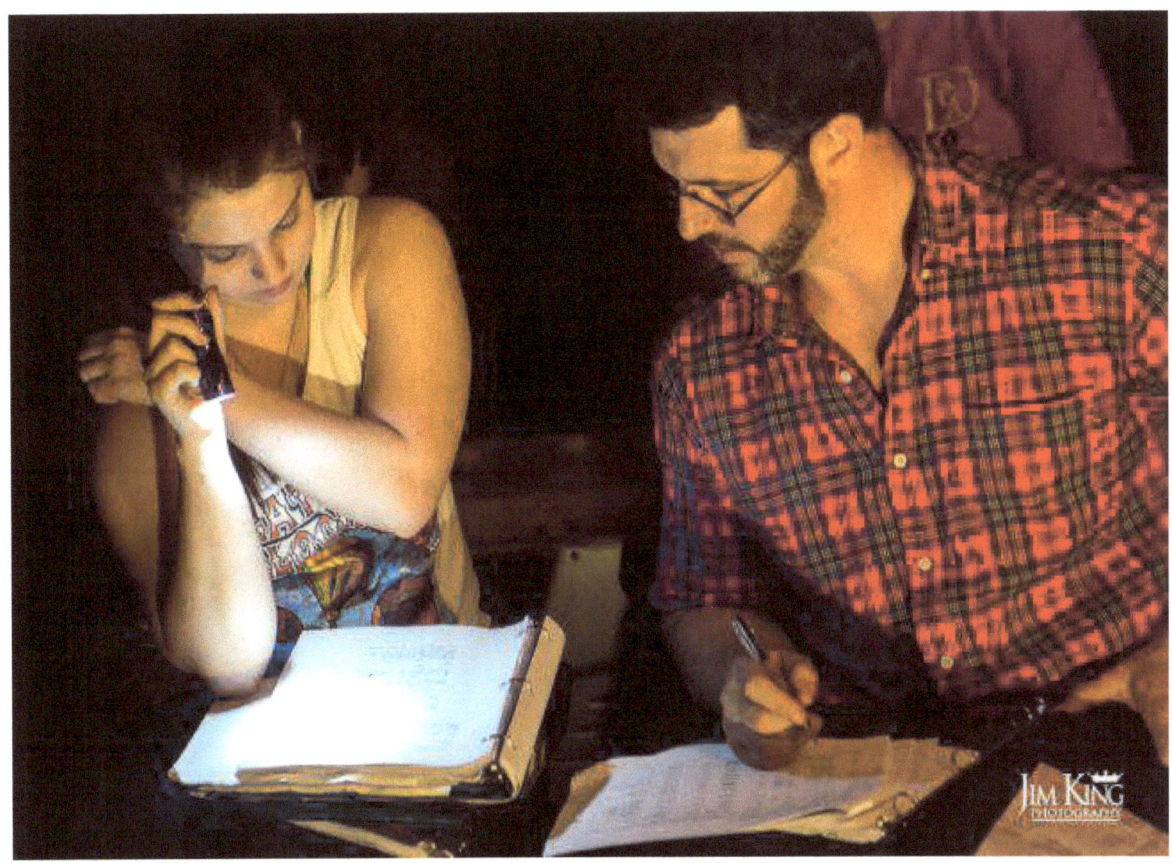

Looking over script with Script Supervisor on a night shoot

STEP 2: PRE-PRODUCTION PLANNING

Okay, so now that you have a screenplay that is realistic to shoot in utilizing my process, next comes the many steps in the pre-production process. Pre-production is just another word for planning. In my experience, the planning period before principal photography takes about 4-5 months. Now this isn't true if you're talking about Hollywood productions. Keep in mind that we are talking about the process that I use, and even my process could take longer. It really all depends on you and who you have helping out in the pre-production process. You may not realize this, but everything that you are about to do to make your film happen is what a producer does. That's right. You will be the producer of this film. You may have help from other producers that you bring on board, but you are the main producer because this is your project.

Section Highlights

1. The key to successful pre-production is efficient planning.
2. Pre-production can take 4-5 months or longer.

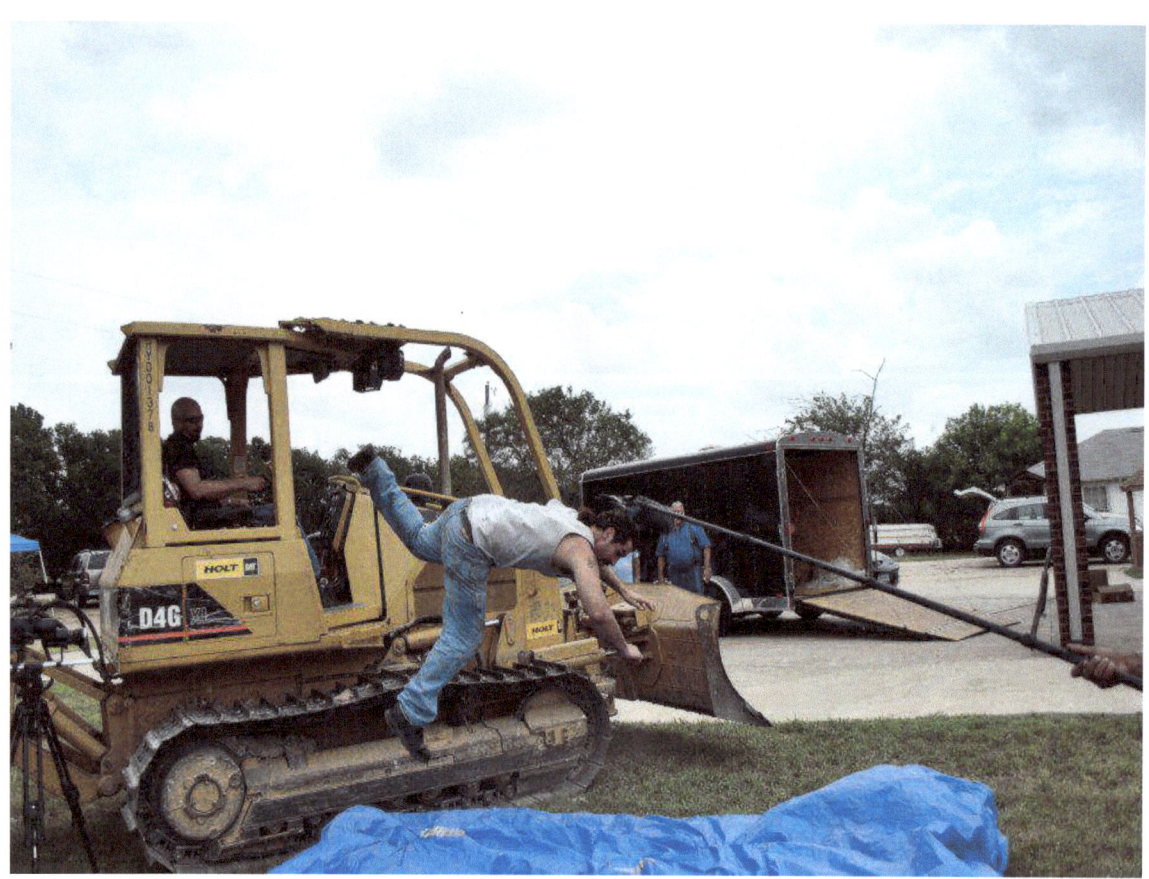

Falling off the bulldozer in "Preacher Man."

STEP 3: NETWORKING

Networking with your friends and other filmmakers is a key ingredient to the success of your film. You can't do it alone, you will need help. In my case, the help came from my friend Stuart who has the same dreams as I do. I couldn't have done this without his help. I think it is important to bring in someone that shares the same vision as you. If you don't have these kind of friends, it will be more difficult but not impossible.

My second film, which is currently in post-production, is called "Something in the Woods." It is basically a true story, according to witness accounts, of how a family in the 1960's dealt with a Sasquatch coming around their home. Now whether or not you believe in Bigfoot is irrelevant, the point I am trying to make is that I brought in one of my close friends to help produce the film alongside Stuart and me. He is involved in a lot of Bigfoot research, and is also an actor. I knew that he could bring a lot to the table in helping me produce this film. Not only could I utilize his connections in the Bigfoot community, but he could also take some of the burden of pre-production off my back.

So in the case of my second film, the first thing I did was to enlist the help of a third producer. I knew that my friend Mike would be happy to be involved in a Bigfoot film if it was on the level and not just another 'B Horror' film. I sent him the script and he loved it. The thing is, I knew Mike's main passion was acting, so to sweeten the deal I gave him a supporting role in the film. I didn't make him audition for the role because I already knew Mike was a great actor. Giving Mike a supporting role now made his producing job much more important. It was a barter type trade, and in the process I am outlining here, bartering is another key ingredient in the recipe. I will discuss bartering later, but for now I want to continue with the importance of networking.

Once you have your producers in place, you will need to be in constant communication with them throughout the whole process. Miscommunication is a like an infectious virus that can slip in and ruin the project before it even gets started. And by the way, remember that you are recruiting people to help you accomplish your vision. You will need to leave your ego at the door. You will be asking a whole lot from people and you will need to be extremely patient with them because more than likely, all these people aren't full-time filmmakers. They have full-time jobs and families that come first. The first moment you are rude or impatient with someone who is trying to help you, you can wave goodbye to that person. It is alright to have disagreements about how to accomplish certain tasks, but always utilize kind words and good communication skills. Mike knew from the start that this was my project and that I was leading, but I never had to tell him that. That didn't keep him from telling me his opinions though. I welcomed his opinions and many times we did things Mike's way because it was the better choice.

Just remember that this project of yours can take off from here or crash land on the runway before it even gets off the ground. How you treat people will be a big determining factor in this. Furthermore, you will have to remain this way throughout the entire process. My goal in making both films was to "be nice." I disagreed with many people and had to take charge several times, but there is a way to do it and a way not to do it. You will need to become a master at controlling your tongue and temper if you expect my process to work for you because your patience with people will be tested twenty times a day, especially once the camera starts rolling. That may not seem very important to you at this point, but trust me, trust me, trust me, you will want to wear a fireman's hat because you will be putting out fires between people on set all the time. It is just something that can't be avoided. So, become a good fireman so to speak. Be ready to serve people and communicate well with everyone you bring aboard your film project!

Section Highlights

1. Networking is key to success. You will need help from others. Recruit reliable

help from a trusted source.

2. Constant communication with other producers is a must.

3. Treat people the right way. An ego will get you nowhere fast.

STEP 4: PRODUCERS ON BOARD

Once you have your producers on board, it is time to devise the plan. You will want to set up a meeting where everyone can get on the same page. You will need to discuss many things, including who will be doing what in terms of dividing up the producer responsibilities. It is important to set realistic goals at the first meeting. The producers will need to set a tentative shoot date as to when you expect to begin filming your movie and how long the filming will take. Of course, you will not know how long the filming will take until someone creates a shooting schedule. Don't worry, it's not as hard as you think it is and I did with no prior experience. I made both of my shooting schedules since I was the screenwriter on both projects. The shooting schedule will be discussed in further detail later. For now, you will need to focus on setting the project goals and what steps the producers will be taking to accomplish them. Other items that need to be discussed are as follows: casting, crew, equipment, sponsorship, fundraising, food for cast/crew, and marketing. I will discuss each of these elements in this outline. Each element is very critical to the success of your film project. Keep in mind that you will wear many hats, as will the other producers. You don't have money to hire production managers, casting directors, extras wranglers, line producers, etc. You and everyone involved will have to help one another and share job duties as needed. You may have several titles on the project, or prefer to have only one title, but you will still have to fill in the shoes of the personnel that you can't afford to hire.

Section Highlights

1. It is important to meet regularly with other producers and stay in constant contact.

2. Be prepared to wear many hats other than just a producer.

STEP 5: GETTING THE WORD OUT

It is almost instantaneous that when you decide to make a movie, word will start to spread. Getting the word out is just another way to describe "marketing." You will tell your friends or family, and they will tell theirs and so forth. Soon, you will have people approaching you through phone calls, Facebook, instant messaging, etc.

My first word of advice here is be prepared for the naysayers and negative people who will doubt you. Don't be offended when you run into negativity. Instead, let it be a motivating factor in your quest. It is never a good idea to argue with people about how you will be the next great filmmaker. I have found that many of these negative people will actually come back later and make a donation when they see that the project is gathering momentum. As word spreads of your upcoming film project, there will be many people who will want to be a part of the project in some way or another. Never turn anyone away if you can help it. Some people will just want to be an "extra" in the film and make some kind of contribution.

There will come a point when you have cast the film that you will have to tell applying actors that the roles are filled, but always treat people with respect. Stepping on people or ignoring them can come back and bite you. It is a small world. "Oh yeah, my daughter wanted to be an extra but you turned her away...and I just happen to be on the city council. I am sorry but I can't help you with closing down the city block for filming." Tread carefully with everyone you come across and meet. Not that you are wanting to get something out of every person you meet, but it's all about networking in the film industry.

The marketing of your film in the beginning is important to build interest around your project. Call the local paper and tell them that you are making a movie in the area. Most newspapers will want to come out and interview you. Include your contact information in the paper so that people who are interested in the project can get in touch with you. The more interest you build in the project, the more help you are likely to receive. So in short, the marketing aspect of your film in the beginning is just as important as the marketing of your film when it is completed.

Section Highlights

1. Start spreading the word about your film through word of mouth and social networks. Let the world know that you are making a movie.

2. Don't fixate on negativity from people who don't believe you can do it, or from anyone that tries to discourage you.

3. Try to involve as many people as possible. Don't turn anyone away if you can help it.

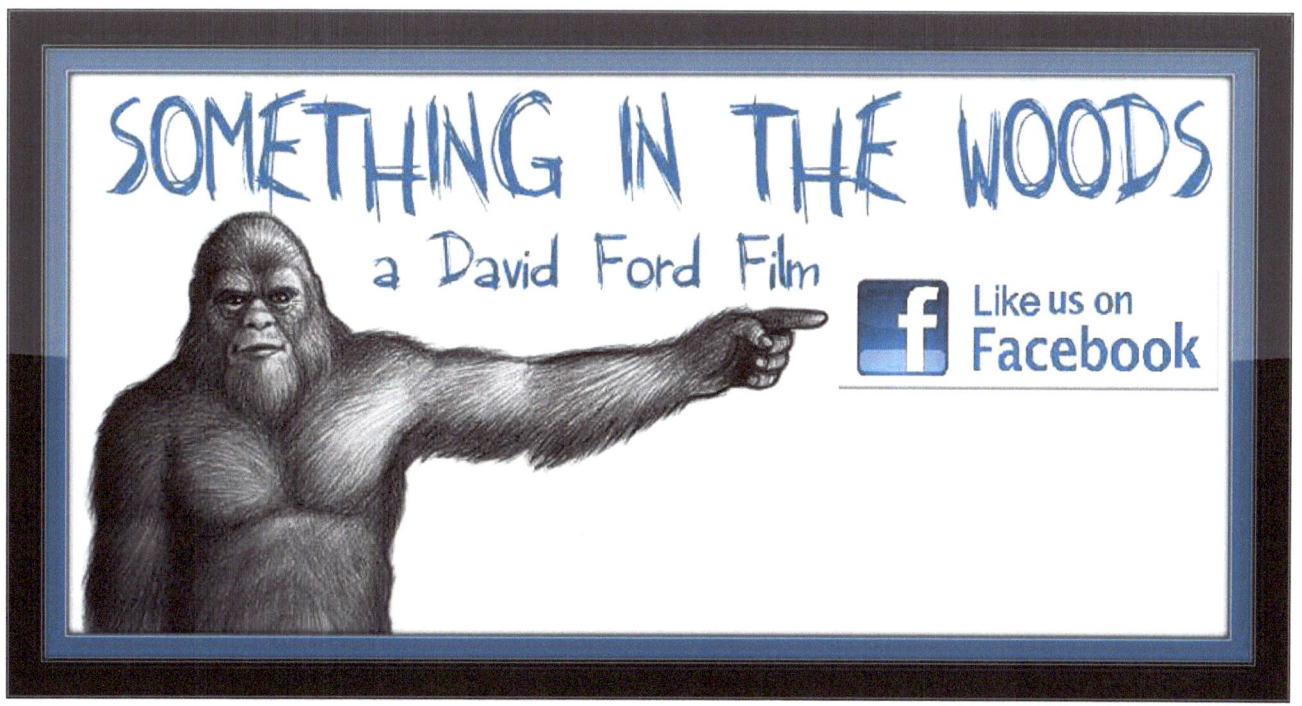

Creating banner ads on Facebook helps promote your film project.

STEP 6: THE SCHEDULE

Before you get too far along, it is best to go ahead and put together a tentative shooting schedule. This will give you direction on how to proceed and what all you will be needing over the course of the film. I had never put together a film schedule before my first film, "Preacher Man." But since I was the writer and since I didn't have money to pay someone, I decided to take a crack at it. Surprisingly, it wasn't that difficult as I had imagined. Don't get me wrong, it is time consuming but it shouldn't take more than a week if you work on it a bit everyday.

If you are the screenwriter it is easier because you know what scenes are going to be easy and what scenes are going to be difficult. You know the story and the characters and can assemble a schedule that warmly embraces the two in the most efficient manner. **NOTE: Remember the schedule comes before friends, actors, or crew preference.** I received so many emails from people asking me if I could adjust the schedule to meet their needs. The answer, "I will try but I can't make any promises.' So what is the big deal with adjusting the schedule for people? It is because one small scene change can often throw off the entire schedule. It isn't always the case but I have found it most often to be true. I have tried to alter schedules only to find myself in a big mess, which has a domino effect of disaster. There are some instances where the change is okay and actually helps the schedule so don't immediately say 'no.' But beware my friend, beware of how adjusting the schedule for people can hurt the project and lengthen it.

So, how do you put together a schedule with no experience? Here are the steps that I utilized when putting together a basic schedule.

Putting Together a Shooting Schedule:

1. **Make a list of all your locations in the script**. Once you have the list, go through them

and group the locations that take place at the same location. For example, seventy percent of my last film took place at an old farm house. So the whole first week of filming we were basically at that one location.

2. **Separate day scenes from night scenes**. Once you get your locations grouped properly, you will want to go in and separate the day scenes from the night scenes. You can shoot day scenes and night scenes in the same day but beware of time constraints. I have found it is easier to schedule my day shots during the day and do all my night shots on a different day. This allows the cast and crew a break when you shoot a long day and plan to shoot a long night shot the next day. They will get some valuable rest and relaxation before gearing up for a night shoot the following day.

3. **Analyze each scene.** While putting together the schedule, it is important to note on every scene what cast members are required for that scene, whether it is an interior or exterior shot, a night or day shot, and what props will be needed. A prop in my book is anything that is needed other than the actors for that particular scene. If you have a scene that requires a cop car to be there, then you better have 'cop car' in the prop list for that day. Another thing to consider in the schedule is time. Don't forget you are making a film where most people have jobs and all your food donations and sponsorships have a clock on them, and the clock is ticking down. In the case with my film, I only had two weeks to film what normally takes a month. If you really spend some time on the schedule then it is possible to accomplish what sometimes seems impossible. It is highly important that your cast/crew understand that your film project is going to be long hours. Our average film day was 12 hours. That is pushing the limits, I know. Yet, I had no choice in my second film because we had to wrap within two weeks or everything would fail because after two weeks there was no more food or lodging. If you get your film made in 2-3 weeks then you are doing good. If you can provide a schedule that allows for a month of filming you are doing awesome.

4. **Don't rush it.** One thing you don't want to do is 'rush' your film. You may be on a tight schedule but if you rush it then it will look like crap in the editing room. Get the shot no

matter how long it takes. This brings me to my second point in making a schedule. You must allow 2-3 days for pick-up shots. There will be days when you are running behind because of technical issues, weather, or sickness. Just do as much as possible on your shooting day and whatever you can't get that day, add those scenes to the pick up shot list at the end of the schedule. Now, there are instances where you can squeeze a pick up shot in the regular schedule. If you get finished one day on time and have an extra hour, then by all means go back and pick up that shot if possible. As you begin to put together the schedule you will find yourself making notes and going back and adjusting it as needed. Once you get the schedule finished, go back and count each scene in the schedule to make sure you haven't left any out by accident. Remember, you will be shooting out of scene sequence so it is easy to accidentally leave out a scene.

5.   **Consider the time of year.** As I said earlier, most people have full time jobs. I was able to shoot my films during the summers because being a teacher, we get off nearly three months for summer break. For me, this was the best choice. I couldn't have done this during the school year when I was teaching. It is hard to shoot in the summer because of the heat, and most people plan their vacations during the summer. Yet, there are many people who are retired or have flexible schedules. If you happen to have a flexible schedule, it is best to shoot at a time of the year where the temperatures aren't extreme. I don't recommend shooting in the dead of winter or summer unless your script calls for such. Yet, you may be in my position and have no choice. Do what you have to do but plan accordingly for the season in which you plan to shoot your film.

Section Highlights

1.   Do not alter the schedule to meet the needs of actors unless you can do so without throwing the schedule off track.

2.   Make a list of the locations and group them together by location.

3.   Figure out what actors and props are needed for each scene.

4.   Analyze the script to see how many day scenes and night scenes there are and

adjust the schedule accordingly.

5. Consider the time of year that you want to shoot and make arrangements for the needs of the cast/crew.

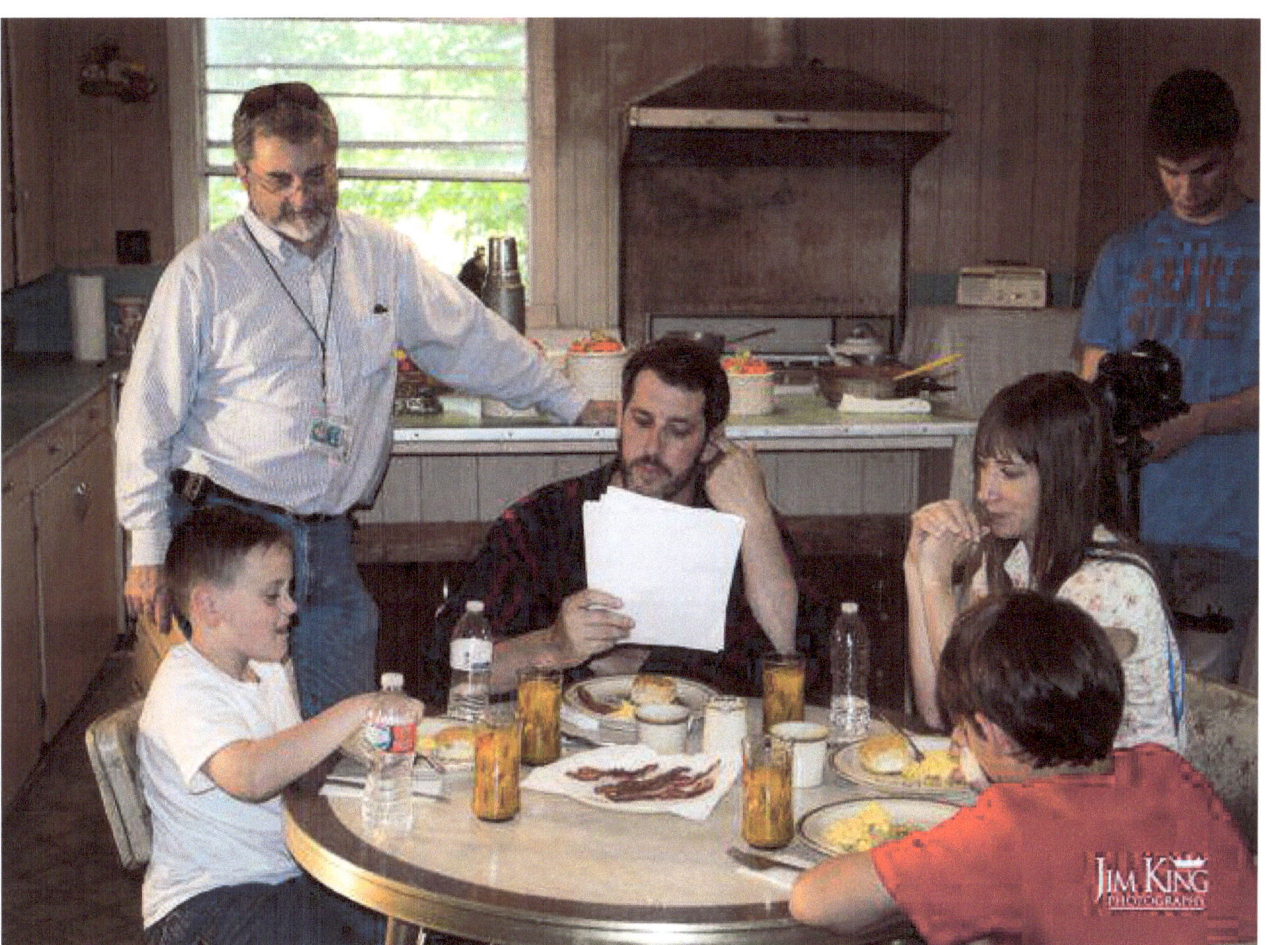

Gearing up for a scene on set of, "Something in the Woods."

STEP 7: THE CONTRACT

Before we go any further, it is time to discuss one of the most important aspects of your film. Earlier, I had mentioned that I had made a very big mistake on my first film. That mistake was with the *contracts*. Let me say this about contracts; "Don't trust anyone when it comes to contracts." The nicest person in the world can literally destroy your film project if you don't get their signature on a contract.

This is what happened on my first project. The first day of filming, the printer went down and I had one particular person that didn't sign. Well, I trusted this person and told them that I could get their signature later, before filming was complete. To make a long story short, that person never signed the contract and to this day, the project is in a legal struggle between attorneys, all because I made the mistake of trusting a 'nice person.' Without a signature from an actor, you can't move forward with your project in distribution because you can be sued for using that person's image without their permission. The person who didn't sign came back at the end of filming and demanded unreasonable rates and even wanted a big percentage of the film in distribution. I tried to reason with this person but all my efforts failed. So now, I have to wait until my attorney can sort it out which who knows how long that could take. That is why having a signed contract from everyone involved is the first thing you must have done before any filming takes place.

Any cast member or crew member that comes aboard your film should sign a contract as soon as possible. This will protect you in a big way. If you don't know anything about putting a contract together, get a sample contract from the net and get a lawyer to look it over and make any needed adjustments for your film. If you are going to do your film the way I did mine, then I must discuss with you another important aspect of this process. It is called a 'deferred rate.'

Section Highlights

1. You can't trust anyone when it comes to contracts. All cast and crew must sign a contract before you begin filming.

2. Unsigned contracts can hold up your film in distribution and can land you in court.

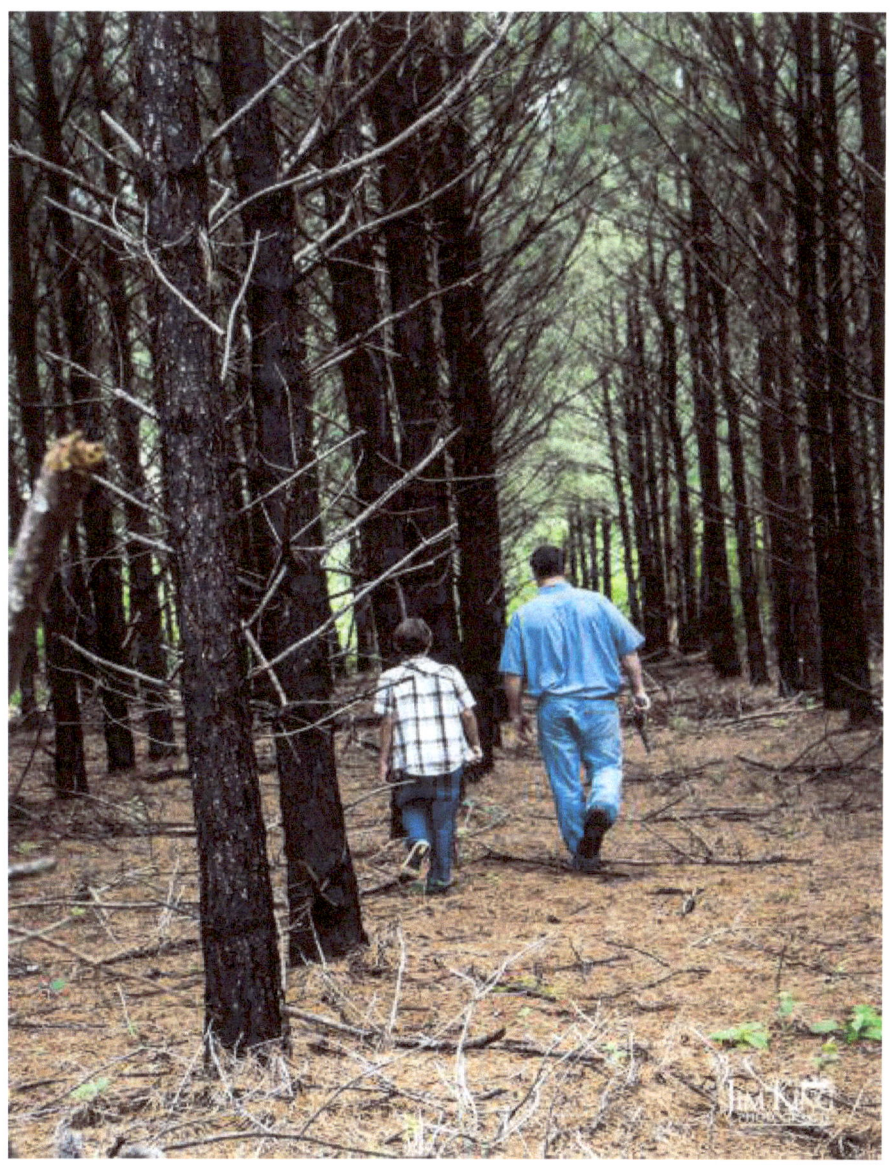

A scene from, "Something in the Woods."

STEP 8: THE DEFERRED RATE

You can go about getting people to work on your project in numerous ways but if you're like me, then you won't be able to pay anyone involved on your film project during filming or after immediately after filming. It is important that your cast and crew know that their hard work isn't for nothing and that one day there is a chance they could be paid for their work on your film project. The 'deferred rate' is the answer here. But beware, because if you don't word it right in the contract then you will have people expecting payment right after the film is complete.

It is critical that everyone aboard your film project understands what a deferred rate means, and you must make it clear in the contract what it means. You must put a clause in the contract that states <u>that no wages will be paid unless the film is successful in distribution and makes the money needed to cover the budget of the film.</u> Yes, your film will have a budget. While it may not cost you a lot of money to make this film, the labor of the cast and crew over the course of your filming coupled with future editing expenses will add up very quickly. Both of my film budgets came close to two hundred thousand dollars. Now don't get confused here; <u>you don't need two hundred thousand dollars to make the film.</u> It is the price of your film once it is complete. I will discuss budget later. For now, let's continue with the deferred rate.

On both my projects, I offered the cast and crew a basic one hundred dollar a day deferred rate deal, which means everybody makes one hundred dollars a day for their work, no matter how many hours you shoot on a particular day. Sometimes you may have to offer key crew members more than this, especially if they will be using their expensive film equipment. In that case, you may offer whatever day rate you choose to that person. Just remember, that will need to be reflected in the individual contract.

To conclude on this important element, I would suggest that whomever you bring on board understands very well that he/she will not be paid unless the film makes back the budget in distribution. Your cast and crew need to understand there is a chance your film will not make a dime and that they may never make any money. But in reality, this is not really a bad thing because this clause actually helps weed out the people who are on your project for the wrong reasons. Making your first movie shouldn't be about the money in the first place. You are trying to show the world what you can do and get your foot in the film community door. Trust me, you want people involved in your project who want to be there no matter what deferred rate you are giving them.

Hopefully, any cast and crew that is involved with your film want to be there and help you make a great movie because like you, they love movie making and want to learn the process of movie making. You will find that many people will do whatever it takes to be apart of your project because you are making a movie and that is something to get excited about. Of course, you will come across some people who don't really think it is a big deal. These are the people that you DON'T want apart of your project. Make sure everyone on board your project thinks it is a privilege to be there.

Section Highlights

1. Make sure your cast and crew understand what a 'deferred rate' means and include a clause in the contract which states that no monies will be paid until the film clears the budget in distribution.

2. The people you bring aboard your project should be there because they love movie making, not because they think it will somehow make them lots of money.

STEP 9:   THE BUDGET

I am not good at putting together a budget but my friend Stuart is. Stuart is the one on my team who put together a budget for both of my films. I have come across people who can't seem to understand you don't need the film's budget sitting in a bank account before you actually make the film. If that was the case, I would have never been able to make a movie. The budget is basically what your film costs to make if you did have hard cash to make it. If a distributor offered a 'buy out' on your project, they will want to see the budget. It is important that your budget accurately reflects all the expenses and rates to make your film.

On my second film project, I had someone say to me, "You're saying it cost two hundred thousand dollars to make this film but I know you didn't have that kind of money." That is a true statement. But what this person failed to realize is that the 200k budget amount is basically what we owe the cast/crew once the film is made. We didn't have two hundred thousand to make the film but that is what it cost when the filming is complete, when all the hours of labor and time sheets are added up. If the film turns out to be a hit, then everyone involved in your film will be paid the daily rate they agreed to in their contract. More simply put, you wouldn't sell your film to a distributor for the small amount of two thousand that you raised to make the film.

I hope this makes sense because there was some confusion on this issue among some of my crew members in the beginning. We had to explain to them that the budget doesn't represent money in the bank but what the film actually cost to make once it is complete. It is the least amount you would sell your film for to a distributor to ensure your cast/crew are paid if the film is a success.

Section Highlights

1. You must have someone put together an accurate budget and keep daily time sheets of all work and expenses to make your film.

2. In a deferred rate scenario, the budget doesn't reflect money in the bank. It is what it cost to make the film once it is complete.

STEP 10: PUTTING THE CREW TOGETHER

Once you have the schedule, you will know how to advertise the positions on your film project, whether for cast or crew. If you are an actor, you probably already have lots of connections locally in the film industry. But, for the sake of me teaching you my process, let us assume that you don't have any connections. So now the question is, how do you find qualified crew to work on your film project?

There are several ways to go about searching for crew. First, you should look locally. Utilize social networks such as Facebook, Linkedin, and Stage 32. A simple posting on these websites will get film crew members messaging you for the details. Also, utilize your state's film commission website. More than likely, you should be able to put out crew calls on the film commission website. **Keep in mind when looking for crew or posting any type of job notice that you remember to include the details about your project.** Make sure you put in capital letters, "DEFERRED RATE" as the pay rate for your film. Even with the capital letters stating that, people will still contact you and ask you about the pay rate.

Another thing to consider when you are looking for crew is to concentrate on filling the most important positions first. Your key positions include: Director, Director of Photography, Assistant Director, Production Manager, Lighting Supervisor, Audio Supervisor, Script Supervisor, and Time Codes Keeper. There are other important crew positions, but these in my opinion are the hardest to find. For example, if you are looking for a Director of Photography, you will need to know if you will want to use their equipment or your own.

The question, "What camera will you be using?" is a question that will come up over and over again. It is best to know the answer to that beforehand. If you don't have any equipment, make a note of that in your job posting for that particular position. Usually, a Director of Photography will have some type of camera. It may not be the best, but if you don't have a camera, it is better than nothing. Also, don't take the first DP that comes along, unless you think he/she is the best person for the job. I made the mistake of selecting a DP too quickly, only to have a more experienced DP with better equipment apply for the position a few days after I signed the first. Remember, you are making an indie guerrilla style film. You most likely will not have all the fancy equipment that large production companies have, but you still need the basics. You need to make sure you have a good camera, good audio, plenty of lighting equipment, steady cam, and such. While assembling your team, make sure you talk with each potential crew member in depth to make sure they understand exactly what to expect on your film set. It is okay to ask someone if they have equipment that can be used on your set. Just be prepared to offer these people a higher rate than the standard one hundred dollars a day.

One trick that can make all the difference in the world on saving time is if you are able to have two cameras rolling on set with each scene. It is sometimes harder to accomplish, but I can't stress enough the value it will bring. Having the ability to knock out two different camera angles on a scene at the same time will save you huge amounts of time.

Section Highlights

1. You should first search locally for a film crew unless you can afford lodging for the ones coming in out of town.
2. Put out job postings for crew on social networks like Facebook, Stage 32, and Linkedin.
3. Concentrate on filing the main crew positions first.
4. If you don't have a good camera to shoot with, make sure you mention this in the job posting. It is possible that a Director of Photography will be willing to use his/her own equipment.

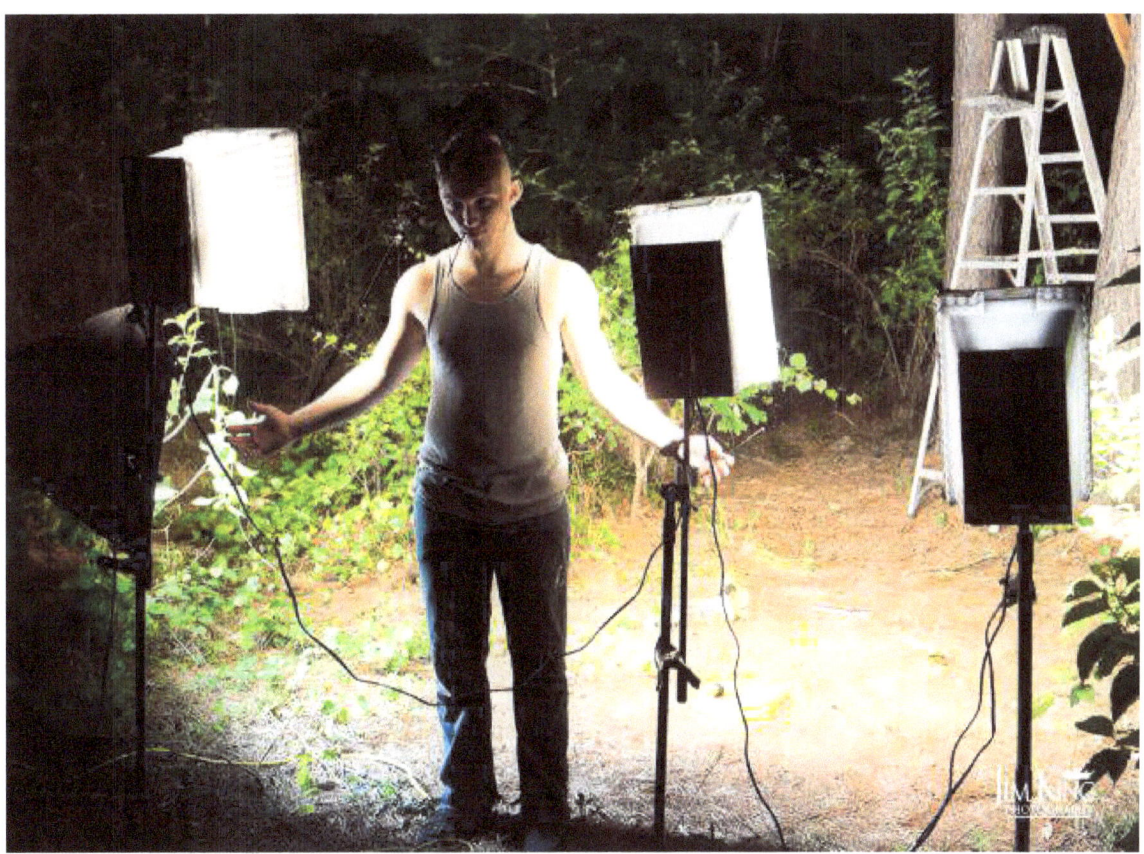

A crew member setting up lights for a night scene

STEP 11: GETTING SPONSORSHIPS AND DONATIONS

Having the schedule completed allows for better planning when it comes to sponsorship and donations. Let's say that it will take 18 days of principal photography. With that in mind, now you will have to provide food and drinks for the cast/crew for those 18 days. That could be expensive if you had to pay for it with cash.

Sponsorships and donations are two key ways that you can fund craft services. It is easy to set-up a fundraiser type of website like "Kickstarter" or the many other websites like it. It is important that you also put some time and effort into making your funding website look its best. The better the website looks, the more interest and donations you will receive. Also, make sure this website has plenty of perks to offer those who make a contribution. We offered shirts, tickets to the premiere, signed photos from cast, etc. Make sure the funding website has at least 40 days to reach your funding goal. **Share the link to your funding website every few days on social networks, while at the same time encouraging your friends and network connections to help support your film endeavor.**

In addition to donations, pursue sponsorships through every avenue possible. When it comes to getting food and other types of sponsorship, you will need to be a good salesman. This is where bartering comes into play in this process of mine. If you walk into a local cafe or restaurant and ask them to sponsor a day or more to feed the cast and crew, they will want to know what they are going to get out of it. You can offer these sponsors advertising through thanking them in the film credits, as well as taking photographs of their establishment and thanking them publically on Facebook. I mention Facebook a lot because everybody and their dog has a Facebook page, and most businesses have a Facebook page also. Social networks will play a huge role in almost every aspect of your film project.

Another thing that really helps is if you inform a potential business sponsor that you plan to show a slide show of all the sponsors at the local premiere of your film. This gives them the opportunity to have their business and workers on the big screen before the premiere. While people are visiting and waiting on the your movie to begin at the cinema, you can have a slideshow of all the sponsors that supported your project. Be prepared for rejection, but don't let a few rejections bring you down. It is also good to have some t-shirts with your film logo that you can offer potential sponsors immediately. I don't know what it is about movie t-shirts, but people love them. You can actually get a discount on t-shirts, or even get a batch of 20 or so donated if you play your cards right. One trick my producer Mike utilized in getting a batch of 50 free t-shirts was offering for the t-shirt shop to put their logo and information somewhere on the shirt, like the back of the shirt or sleeve. This helps advertise their business, so there is a good chance a shop will be willing to do this. Basically, when it comes to getting sponsorships and donations, the sky is the limit. Don't be afraid to ask everyone for support!

The second way to raise funds is through fundraising events. There are all kinds of things you can do to raise money. You can do a bake sale, silent pie auction, or live music with food. You will need help on this from the other producers so don't try to shoulder the burden alone. Get everyone involved that you can. You will be surprised at how many people will be willing to help you at these events. These are just a few ways to get you going in the right direction. Heck, you may even have a wealthy friend that may want to invest in your project for a small percentage of any future profits of the film. The point is, don't limit yourself. Use any and all methods available to get food, drinks, and basic production costs covered.

Section Highlights

1. Utilize the schedule to determine the exact number of days that you will need sponsorship.

2. Set-up a fundraising page like Kickstarter that allows for contributions in exchange for perks. There are many types of these websites on the net. Make sure to explore the pros and cons of each before deciding on which to go with.

3. You will have to be a good salesman in order to get businesses to sponsor or donate to your project. Have something to barter with, even if it is a shirt with your movie logo on it. Don't let rejection get you down. It will happen but you

must keep trying. Some will help and some will not.

4. Put together one or more fundraising events and get everyone that you can involed. Advertise the events on all of your social networks like Twitter and Facebook.

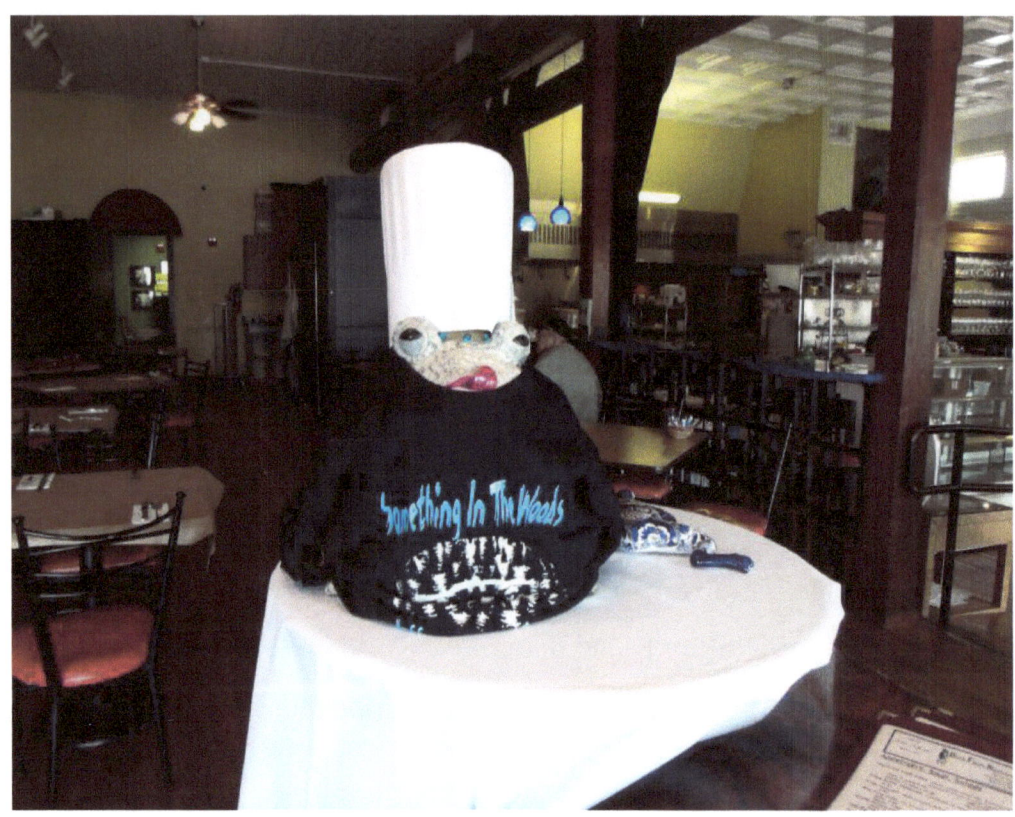

A restaurant sponsor proudly displays our film shirt on it's frog mascot.

STEP 12: CASTING YOUR FILM

On both of my film projects, I did the casting. There is no shortage of actors out there. Simply put, there are plenty of good actors who will work on your project for a deferred rate. It is obvious that any actor you bring on board will be unrecognizable and unknown in the film industry. I mention that because you will come across actors with big egos, who will ask for more than what you are willing to give. I tend to avoid these types of people because there are plenty of others who will be willing to do the job for what you are offering.

So, what are you offering to actors on your project? You are offering copy, credit, meals, and deferred pay. Don't offer lodging if you can't afford to do so. Make sure the job posting for casting states that actors must be able to work "local hire." You can make exceptions as you need, especially for the lead characters. You can have actors come audition for you or you can have them send you a taped audition, or even watch their demo reel.

When it comes to "Extras Casting," you will need to put someone in charge because you will not have time to deal with film extras on set. The way I handled it was to get a close friend to be my "Extras Casting Director." Essentially, this person handled putting out a post in the local paper stating the shoot dates that extras would be needed, and took their information as they applied. The Extras Casting Director will need to form a database of everyone who applies, and then call each one a day or two before they are needed on set to confirm.

With regard to wardrobe and make up, since you may not be able to have that available on set, you will need to make sure all the actors bring 3-4 sets of clothes to set that you can choose from and approve. It is best to do this before the filming begins. We had make-up on some days for both of my films, but it wasn't consistent because these people are usually hard to find for a deferred rate. Instead of counting on having this position filled, have your actors get a base powder and simply apply it before their scene. It's not Hollywood style, but it will work.

Lastly, make sure actors know the schedule and are completely available. They should not have any other commitments during the filming of your project because as with any movie, the schedule can and will change. It may be a slight change but it can cause problems if an actor has a doctor's appointment the day they are needed.

Section Highlights

1. Stay away from actors with egos. Make sure actors understand what you're offering on your film project. There are plenty of good actors who will do great work for what you are offering.

2. Have someone else besides yourself be in charge of 'Extras Casting.' You will not have time to deal with this during pre-production.

3. Make sure the actor doesn't have any prior commitments during the schedule because they schedule could change slightly during filming.

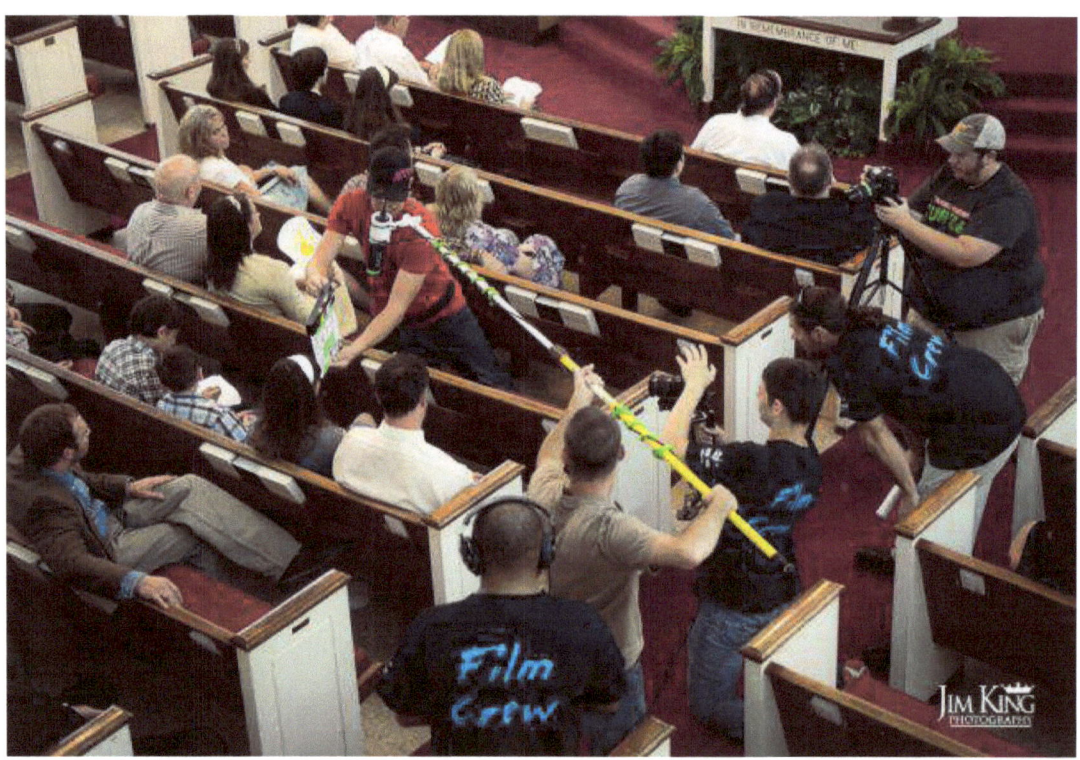

A scene from 'Something in the Woods' that required extras.

STEP 13: COMMUNICATION

If your film production is the cake, communication is the icing on the cake. Good communication from the very beginning of your project is a major key ingredient for success. Even your best efforts in communication will sometimes still fall short. But don't kick yourself because communication sometimes falls between the cracks on a film set, despite your best efforts.

Once you have your cast and crew, you will need to immediately set up a production email. Do not use your own personal email because it looks unprofessional. Set up the production email and email everyone involved in the project, and then make sure everyone responds back to you to confirm their receipt. It is a good idea to ask everyone for their information in the first email along with a recent head shot. You will need their head shots for future marketing purposes, especially when you have an official website with cast and crew photos and interviews.

Once you establish an email system, be sure to communicate regularly with the cast crew, at least once a week prior to filming. Keep everyone involved up to date and on what is going on in the pre-production process. Again, make sure you set up a Facebook page for your movie and have an official administrator over it to make sure all negativity or inappropriate posts are deleted quickly. Having a movie Facebook page or Twitter account has been two of our best resources thus far in spreading the word about our film. The movie page will need to be updated regularly to keep people interested and to generate more 'likes.' So, the main thing with communication is to make sure you are doing it and doing it well. If communication becomes an issue, people will start dropping out of your project.

Section Highlights

1. Good communication is a key ingredient for success on your project.
2. Once your cast and crew is in place, set up a production email immediately

and communicate with everyone involved in the project on a weekly basis.

STEP 14: PRE-PRODUCTION ESSENTIALS

There are some importance elements that will make your life easier when it comes to filming your project. I have made a list to help you along on these essential aspects. They are in no particular order of importance.

1. **Locations:** Make sure you have all your locations secured before filming and have back up locations ready for the main location shoots in case one location falls through on you.

2. **Scenes:** Determine the really tough shots in the schedule and make adjustments for them. If you have a tough scene that could take half a day to shoot, allow for it. Don't cram other scenes around it or you will end up rushing the scene and not get the best shots.

3. **Props:** Make a list of all the props that you will need for your film and start working on obtaining each prop. You don't want to be already filming and looking for props. Trust me, it's a time killer and often you will have to re-write a scene if you can't find the exact prop needed for a particular scene.

4. **Photography:** Find someone to take photos for the film, which is called a 'Stills Photographer.' I was blessed on my second film to get a professional photograher. He took about two thousand photos in two weeks and they were so beautiful. I can't stress the importance of getting good photos for scenes. It will help in the marketing and promotion of your film, allow for future sources of revenue, give your film production value, and help you in the area of continuity.

5. **Meetings:** Have at least two meetings with key crew before production begins to make sure your team are on the same page. Remember, this goes back to good planning.

6. **Schedule:** Put the schedule under the microscope to make sure everything is as it should be. You want to make sure the schedule is created to maximize time, or rather to save time. Time will be your biggest obstacle and it will never cut you any slack.

7. **Table Read:** Make sure you have a meeting with the cast and have a table read if possible. You want to make sure your actors are fully prepared when they show up to set.

8. **Communication:** Even though you will assigning people to do different jobs, don't automatically assume these people are doing those jobs. You will need to check with them weekly to make sure things are getting done. Just remember, be polite and nice. If you are rude or arrogant, most likely they will not want to work with you.

9. **Planning Shots:** Make sure to get with your Director of Photography routinely to discuss the shooting script. You and the DP will need to collaborate on a daily shot list. This will save lots of time instead of just trying to wing it on set. If you know someone who can storyboard that would also come in handy.

10. **Key Crew:** Make sure that the key crew positions are filled by capable people. They may not have lots of experience but they need to be able to perform the job duty assigned. For example, don't assign someone to do an important task such as 'Time Codes' if they are not dependable or highly detailed and organized.

11. **Job Duties:** Everyone involved must understand their job responsibilities as well as the job responsibilities of others. There will be people who overstep their boundaries and may need to be reminded of their title. Some of this can be avoided if you have everyone introduce themselves and their title at the production meeting. You will also have 'wannabe directors' who want to offer their creative advice on every scene, and how you could do it better. I am not saying never listen to people, but if you have that happening a lot then it will cause much frustration and slow down your film. Trust me, people will try to

overstep their boundaries and when they do, be nice but remind them that the director is in charge of the scene. While there may be plenty of other things to make pre-production go smoothly, these are some of the top items that come to mind. During pre-production, you will sleep and eat pre-production elements. You will constantly be wondering, "Am I forgetting something?" This is a good thing. Always be thinking ahead of what you can do to make sure your project is ready to shoot when the time comes.

Section Highlights

1. Make sure locations are secured with back-ups in mind.
2. Create a list of all props needed and start working on attaining them two months before filming begins.
3. Have regular meetings with cast and crew; keep everyone updated and involved.
4. Everyone involved should know their job title and the title of others involved.

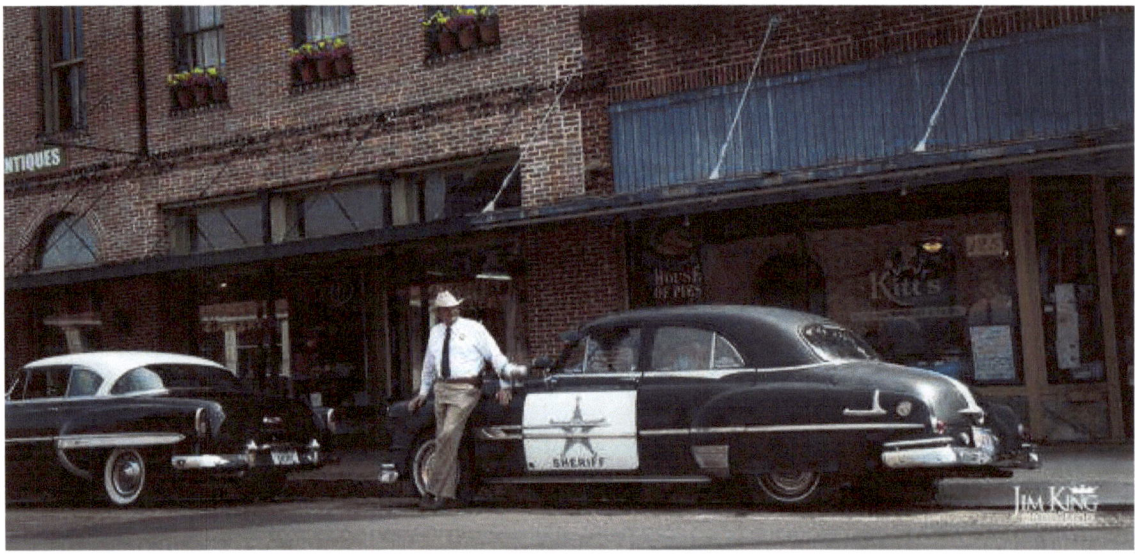

A cast member waits by his prop car in a scene from 'SITW'

STEP 15: PRINCIPAL PHOTOGRAPHY

Once you have accomplished all the above steps in pre-production, you will now be ready to begin shooting your film. Now the real fun begins. Everything you have been working towards for the last few months is now at hand and on the line. You can't let your guard down.

For me, I was the executive producer, writer, director, and lead actor; I had my hands full. You will need help if this is the case with your project. It is not easy to be concentrating on your lines and having to deal with food issues or other things that come up daily on the set. I had to make sure everyone understood to go to the production manager for all issues, and if it was something of major concern then the production manager would come to me. \

Now, if you are not the lead actor then you will have more room to supervise and make sure everything is running smoothly. Each day of production should be like clock work. You'll be moving from one scene to the next in the schedule. Some will be much easier to shoot than others. Your cast and crew will need breaks but don't dillydally too much between breaks or you will soon discover that you are far behind schedule. There are lots of people who will want to 'shoot the breeze' with you when your rushing to the restroom or rushing to grab a drink, so be prepared! Having a good number of production assistants will really make a huge difference in your project. We constantly had production assistants running to get water or drinks to bring to the cast and crew. When it comes to principal photography, here are some important elements, in no particular order, that will help ensure your project will be a success.

Important Elements:

1. Make sure the production manager is sending out 'Call Sheets' every day through the production email.
2. If your shooting at a 'hard to find' location, there should signs on the road and detailed directions to the shoot location.

3. At the end of every day, your footage must be dumped onto a hard-drive and backed up. The worst thing that can happen on your project is to loose many scenes because the footage was not properly handled at the end of the day.

4. You must have your production manager or someone be in charge of watching all the footage that is dumped each day. Our production manager sat in an air conditioned trailer and was looking at footage as it came in on the cards. This is very important so that you can make sure the footage is good. It is very hard to go back and re-shoot scenes at a later date. We had to re-shoot a couple of scenes because we realized there were some scenes that were slightly out of focus. This was very frustrating to find out when your gearing up for another scene. This can be avoided by using monitors during shooting. If you are simply trusting the eye of your DP or camera operator without looking at a monitor during the scene, then it is very easy to miss slight blurs and background issues.

5. Make sure the administration on your project understands not to go out and purchase something and expect to be reimbursed if you have not approved the purchase of an item. I ran into this problem a few times and it can cause problems. If you need an extra case of water, send someone to get it with the money raised from your budget. Don't say, "Can someone go get a case of water?" because if you do, ten people will go buy water and now you owe ten people water money.

6. Be prepared for long days on set. I often made the mistake of pushing my cast and crew too far. Theoretically, your shooting days should be about 10-12 hours. If you go beyond this, which sometimes you have to, don't make it a habit. And if you happen to have a 15 hour day, don't expect people to be there bright and early the next morning. You had better give them some time to sleep in and recover or run the risk of key crew or cast not showing up any more.

7. You must have a holding place for extras and cast that is comfortable with central air. On my last film, I had to buy a portable AC at Lowe's to cool down a room

for cast and crew. You don't want people standing around outside in the heat or cold. It is also a good idea to get a porta-potty on set at your main location unless you have plenty of restrooms there. The main thing here is that you want people to be comfortable and not miserable on set. Keep them happy and have plenty of snacks and drinks available. If you don't, be prepared for complaints and people walking off your project.

8. Be nice and professional. This is highly, highly important. I know I may seem redundant and have mentioned this many times in this booklet, but it is a must. You must be the leader because everyone will be looking to you for morale and motivation. If you start complaining it will trickle down and everyone will start complaining. If you are rude to someone, other people will be rude to other people because they think it is okay if you are doing it. My goal on both films was to never be rude or impersonal with anyone. Even when problems come up, remember that *a kind word turns away a wrathful tongue*. You will need to praise people for their efforts consistently, everyday. People love to feel they are needed and appreciated and remember, they are there because they believe in you, in your project.

9. Treat everyone the same. Do not act like you are above people. Make time when possible to greet people. Take time to sign an autograph for a kid or shake hands with an extra. If you treat people right, they will do you right and can significantly have a positive impact on your project through 'word of mouth.' They will tell their friends and family how nice and cool you were to meet or work with.

Section Highlights

1. The production manager must send out daily call sheets through the production email.

2. Footage must be dumped properly and files backed-up at the end of every

shooting day.

3. Be prepared for long days on set but don't push your cast and crew too hard.

4. Provide a 'holding' place for extras and cast that has central heat. They don't need to be out just standing in the background while you are trying to shoot a movie.

5. Treat everyone with dignity and respect.

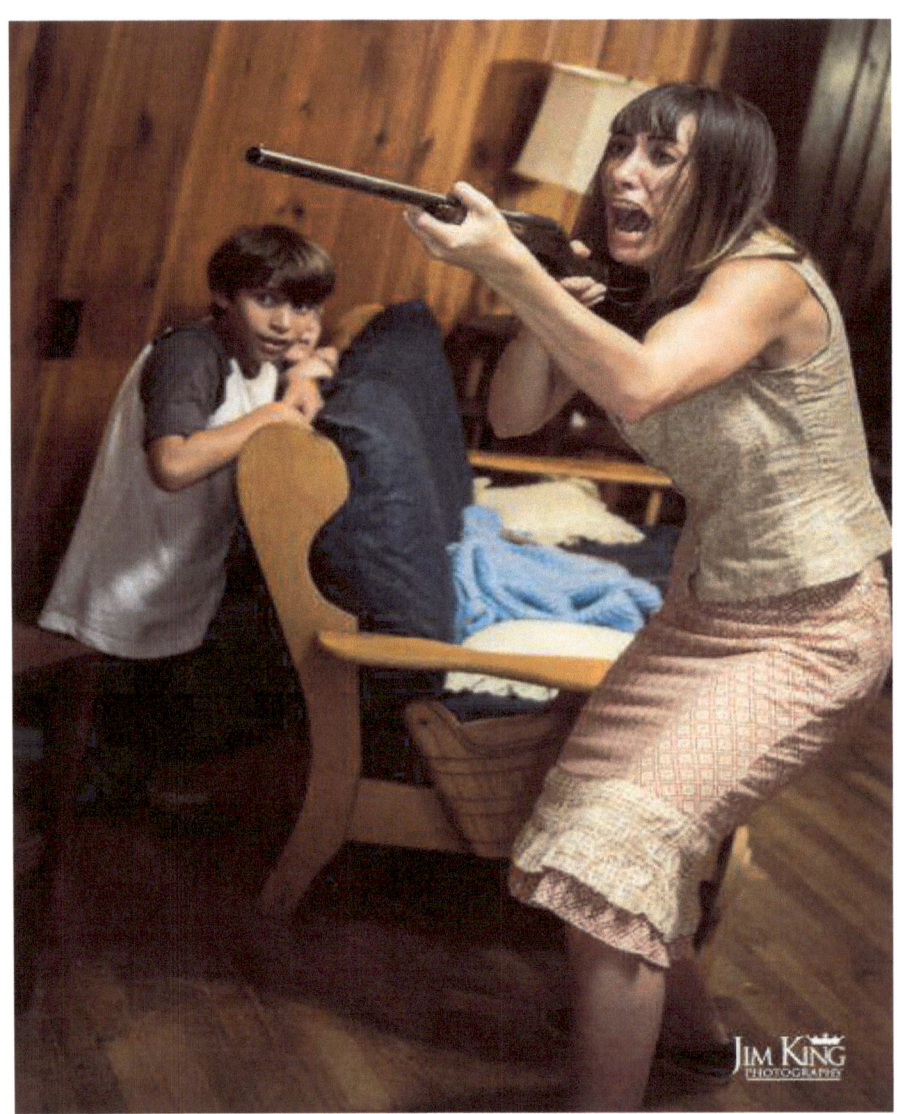

The lead actress on 'Something in the Woods' in an intense moment.

STEP 16: POST PRODUCTION

Congratulations! You did it! But don't go patting yourself on the back just yet because there is still much work to do. Now you have to find a good editor. The editor will need to live close enough so that you or your director can go through the footage and put together a 'rough cut.' Editing is very time consuming and can be very expensive. It will be difficult to find someone that is a good editor to edit your film on a deferred rate. The reason for this is because it is a full time job and takes about two months to piece together a rough cut, and sometimes longer. Not many people can commit to that without being paid for their time.

So how do you go about getting your film edited if you don't have any money? Well, you will have to do some more fund raising if you don't have 4-5 grand laying around, which is what you can probably get it edited for if you find the right person. Don't get me wrong here, it may be possible to find someone to edit your film for a deferred rate if they are independently wealthy or retired, etc. Worst case scenario, if you are a quick learner, you can take a two week crash course in basic editing with Adobe Premier and put together a rough cut yourself.

If you look long and hard, you will find the right person. There are always student editors to consider also or editor that are looking to break into the film industry who will be willing to cut you a deal. Just be careful, a bad editor can destroy your project. I suggest seeing samples of their work first. Regardless of who you choose, you or the director will need to be with the editor as much as possible to ensure the editor is choosing the best takes and angles that accomplish your vision.

Once you get a rough cut, have the editor put together a short 'unofficial' teaser trailer that you can show to the cast and crew at cast/crew party. You can even post on your Facebook page as well as your film website. You will want to keep interest alive in your project all the way from it's completion till release. You can do this several ways. One way is to release a batch of production photos and behind-the-scenes photos every week on social networks. Another way is to do interviews with the cast and crew and post those interviews on the same social networks. You will be surprised how doing these simple things will not only keep the interest alive but also generate much interest in your film.

How you proceed after your film is complete will be up to you. You may plan to put your project into the film circuit or self distribute. There are lots of routes to take once your film is fully complete and ready to show the world. But the first thing you will want to do once your film is complete is to have a premiere locally where the film was primarily shot. Invite the newspaper to come take photos and get the word out.

Now you can pat yourself on the back because you have accomplished your goal. You have made a feature length movie. Whether that movie succeeds or fails just depends on you, but regardless of the success or failure of the film, now you understand the process much better because you went through it. This experience would have been one of the best experiences of your life or one of the worst. As for me, making my two films was the best experiences of my life. I plan to continue making movies and hopefully become a recognizable filmmaker and actor one day.

Section Highlights

1. Once you have completed principle photography on your film, you will need to find an editor that either you or your director can work closely with.
2. Understand that an editor can 'make or break' your project. You will need to choose an editor very wisely.

CONCLUSION

As I stated in the beginning, I don't promise everyone who uses this guide complete success. That all depends upon the person and how committed that person is to making a movie. But I will say what I have given you is a step by step guide that I have used twice, and both times it has worked for me. If you really dream of making a movie and you are committed to it, then I have no doubt that you will succeed. I didn't have anyone telling me what to do and what not to do when I made my first film. I learned from doing it and making plenty of mistakes along the way. I am hoping to spare you some of those same mistakes through the creation of this guide. I truly hope that you find this booklet helpful in your efforts to become a filmmaker. Good luck to you and may God bless your endeavors!

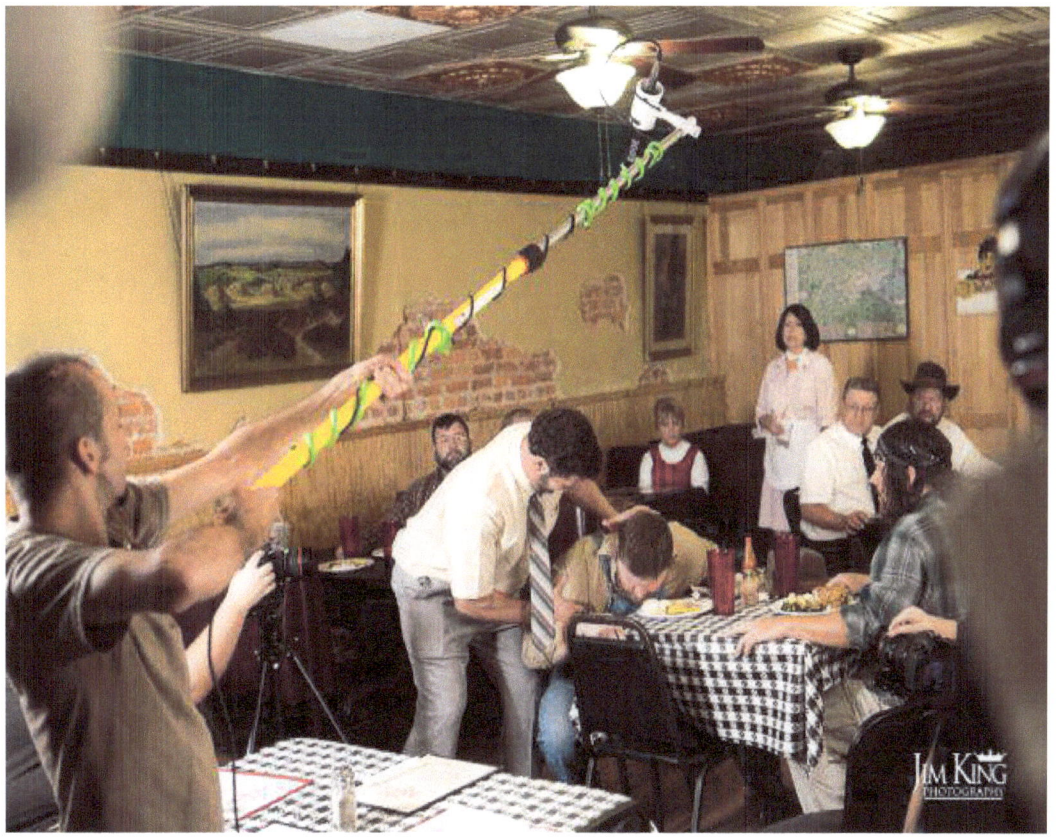

The cafe fight scene on 'Something in the Woods."

MY REFERENCES / LINKS

I have provided a couple of links that you can view. Remember that my first film, "Preacher Man" is not currently listed on IMDB because it is in legal but my second film is listed, "Something in the Woods."

1. MY IMDB PAGE: **http://www.imdb.me/davidford**

2. MY 'Something in the Woods' Facebook page
   https://www.facebook.com/pages/Something-In-The-Woods/650933964971755

**It is probably easier to just type in, "Something in the Woods' on Facebook if the link isn't click-able.

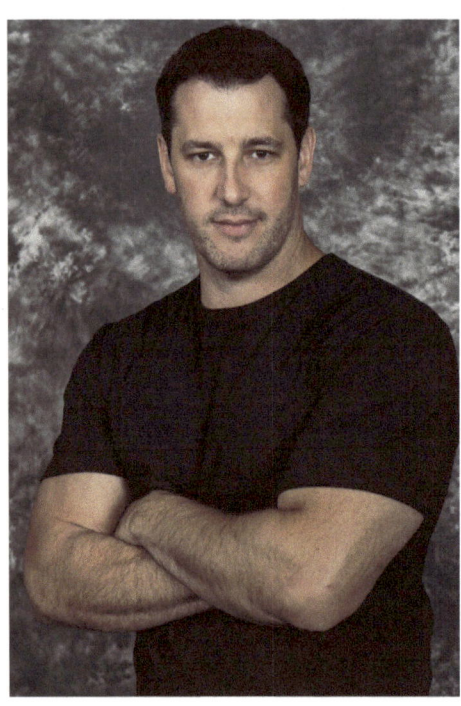